A Gift From God

Copyright © 1994 by Educational Publishing Concepts, Wheaton, Illinois

Published in Nashville, Tennessee, by Thomas Nelson, Inc., Publishers, and distributed in Canada by Word Communications, Ltd., Richmond, British Columbia.

Scripture quotations are from the Contemporary English Version. Copyright © 1991, American Bible Society.

ISBN 0-7852-7977-6

Printed in the United States of America.

1 2 3 4 5 6 7 — 00 99 98 97 96 95 94

My Child You Are...

A Gift From God

by Janet Chillingworth
Illustrated by Priscilla Burris

OLIVER
NELSON

THOMAS NELSON PUBLISHERS
Nashville • Atlanta • London • Vancouver

My child you are…
unique in your own way,
amazing me with the
things you do and say.

*"You are the one who put me
together inside my mother's body,
and I praise you because of the
wonderful way you created me."*

—Psalm 139:13-14

My child you are…
a gift of love, sent from God above.

*"Children are a blessing and a gift
from the LORD."*

—PSALM 127:3

My child you are…
   delighted by the smallest detail,
a snowflake, a spider's web,
   or the trail of a snail.

*"Even the hairs on your head are counted.
So don't be afraid! You are worth much
more than many sparrows."*

—LUKE 12:7

My child you are…
humble and pure,
an example to all of us,
that is for sure.

"But if you are as humble as this child, you are the greatest in the kingdom of heaven."

—Matthew 18:4

My child you are...
in need of affection and praise,
to build strong character
and your self-esteem to raise.

*"Say the right thing at the right time
and help others by what you say."*

—EPHESIANS 4:29

My child you are…
part Mommy,
part Daddy, from head to toe,
each day I watch you
change and grow.

*"So the child grew and became
strong in spirit."*

—LUKE 1:80 NKJV

My child you are…
an investment in the future,
your eager mind I will
thoughtfully nurture.

*"Keep your minds on whatever is true,
pure, right, holy, friendly, and proper.
Don't ever stop thinking about what is
truly worthwhile and worthy of praise."*

—PHILIPPIANS 4:8

My child you are…
full of trust as you sleep,
knowing your life
in safety I'll keep.

"You can be sure that the LORD will protect you from harm."

—PROVERBS 3:26

My child you are…
a privilege to mold,
teaching you lessons
to use 'til you're old.

"Teach your children right from wrong, and when they are grown they will still do right."

—Proverbs 22:6

My child you are…
full of energy as you play,
enjoying the activities
of each and every day.

*"I know the best thing we can do is
to always enjoy life."*

—ECCLESIASTES 3:12

My child you are…
a precious treasure,
and I give thanks for you
without measure.

*"Whatever happens, keep thanking
God because of Jesus Christ.
This is what God wants you to do."*

—1 THESSALONIANS 5:18

My child you are…
   a package of laughter and smiles,
bringing joy to loved ones
   across the miles.

"Happiness makes you smile."

—Proverbs 15:13

My child you are…
  imaginative, releasing creative power,
enjoying your exciting world,
  hour by hour.

"So God created humans to be like himself;
he made men and women."

—GENESIS 1:27

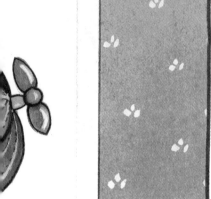

My child you are…
a bright spot in my life,
bringing happiness
through the trials
of everyday life.

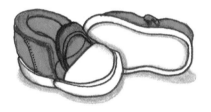

"Let every living creature praise the LORD."

—PSALM 150:6